THE TIME WASTE
MANA(

"This book will help you get things done, making you more productive and successful in life."

Mojo Obadina

The Time Waster's Guide to Time Management

First published in Great Britain in 2021 by

Mo's Mojo Media (UK)

www.unleashyourbusinessmojo.com

ISBN: 978-0-9955489-1-6 (paperback)

A CIP catalogue record for this book is available from the British Library

Book design by Mo's MOJO Media (UK)

Dedication

This book is dedicated to the memory of my loving brother Femi Obadina, whose life was cut short at the young age of 27. You will remain in our hearts and memory forever. Sun re aburo mi!

CONTENTS

Acknowledgements

As I reflect on the scale of this project, I am reminded of the collaborative effort of those who worked tirelessly behind the scenes to help me make my goal of writing this book become a reality.

Firstly, I would like to thank my parents for the values they instilled in me, their love and unwavering support over the years.

To my amazing children, Dami and Tumi, your love is my strength and your presence in my life makes the journey worthwhile and inspires me to be the best role model that I can be. To my parents, who inspire me to be more.

To my editor Alison, who was the first person to see my original manuscript. Her input and attention to detail transformed my work into a great reference book for those who are looking to make their time count.

To my social media family and to all my clients and students – I have learned so much from you and acknowledge your participation in this work.

To all those who inspired me to follow my dreams by living theirs – Oprah Winfrey, Anthony Robbins, Maya Angelou, Richard Branson.

And finally, thank you to those who have supported me on my journey, you all helped me to get my MOJO working. It's impossible to thank everyone but I am forever grateful to you – my friends, family and my community.

Praise for The Time Waster's Guide to Time Management

"What I love about this book is the fact that it isn't just aimed at one group in 'society' but for all, from students to top management. Even mothers at home will take so much from it as it gets you forward thinking but more importantly ACTIONING which is what I'm all about. A recommended read for sure."

Stella Da Silva - International trainer.

"I cannot imagine how challenging it would have been to distil the experiences of effectively managing time and getting organised, but I do know that Mojo does it with a finesse that only a talented author like herself possibly could."

"If you have ever wondered how to connect the dots that will transport you to your destiny and avoid procrastination then I feel like this is an unflinchingly honest place to start."

Councillor Sanchia Alasia.

"A book that keeps the reader in mind and delivers on the promise to help you organise your life!"

Giulia Remondino, M.D Genius in 21 days.

"This book changed my life!! I was able to dive deeper into the root cause of procrastination and by following Mojo's tips I am now healed! A must-read if you want to break the chains of feeling overworked and overwhelmed!"

Antonella Maccianti, Final year student, London South Bank University.

About The Author

Mojo Obadina, the CEO of the brand, Unleash Your Business MOJO!, is an award winning business coach and a university lecturer. Mojo is an inspirational leader who is committed to helping her students and clients to understand what it takes to be successful in business.

In this book, she shares some of her struggles and also the solutions that she has used to gain quick and small wins which is all you need to get results. In this no holds barred manual, she is honest about her failures and is confident that, if she can do it, so can you! So, stop reading and get straight into it. It's a short book but packed with information to get you started straight away.

She has also featured in various publications and on TV as a subject matter expert. Mojo has a powerful presence on LinkedIn, Facebook and on YouTube where she offers thought provoking content on business development in a rapidly changing economic environment.

"Failing to plan is planning to fail." ~ Benjamin Franklin

In her spare time, Mojo plays golf and enjoys roller-skating. She also contributes her time to local organisations by mentoring and supporting entrepreneurial talent.

Preface

I am so happy to be sharing my experiences and knowledge with you.

I have been intending to write this book for months. Why am I actually doing it now? Is it because I finally found some uncommitted time? Wrong. I have assignments to grade, emails to send, new modules and courses to develop and overdue library books to finish reading. I am working on this book now as a way of not doing any of those things :)

As you can guess, this book was actually inspired by my own issues with time management and getting things done. I know that my experience is similar to that of a lot of people out there so I hope this book will in some way motivate and inspire you to get going – after all life is short and we must be able to take full advantage of the time that we have.

We must make it count. Remember - you don't have to work every hour of the day, but the hours you do work must count for something so, if that's four hours of work in a day for you, so be it. It's better to do four hours of work consistently, every day, than spend a whole week doing nothing due to procrastination or paralysis by analysis. Trust me, I once was that person!

The reason procrastination is an important issue is that it can rob you of your future and your success. What you spend your time doing now will be reflected in the future.

So, the question is, "What are you doing now to make sure that your future self will thank you for?"

List 10 things that you have done in the last 24 hours. Keep it somewhere safe and we will revisit this later.

Thanks for choosing to read this book. I would also appreciate and value your constructive comments and honest feedback, so do email me at hello@unleashyourbusinessmojo.com or via social media.

Introduction

The Child in Us.

There are certain problems that are at the root of procrastination, with some of these going back to our childhood. As children, many of us were not encouraged to make mistakes, instead we were corrected a lot more than we needed to be and with those corrections came negative words and phrases like 'You're silly!', 'You're stupid!', 'Why did you do that?' or 'You should know better!' All the should'ves and could'ves. Now we're older, those negative experiences stop us from actually doing anything because we all feel that we are going to be judged. We find ourselves asking the question, 'Am I really good enough?' According to studies done by Erik Erikson[1], it was found that children between the ages of one and three have better positive self-esteem when they are supported to make their own decision regardless of whether they are right or wrong. If they are consistently made to feel ashamed about making mistakes, then they will start believing themselves to be 'stupid'.

Studies show that to condemn and to pick out the annoying behaviour and the difficult aspects of one's character always makes a person worse. It starts with our upbringing. As Desi Williamson writes in his book *Get Off Your Assets!: How to Unleash the Power in You*[2], by the time we reach the age of 18, we've heard the word 'no' 200,000 times, seen 30,000 acts

---

[1] *Erik, Erikson, 1998 The Life Cycle Completed. P.W. W. Norton & Company Publishing*

[2] *Williamson, Desi, 1996 Get Off Your Assets!: How To Unleash The Power In You, Kendall/Hunt Publishing.*

of violence and have received more than 12 million messages in the form of advertising telling us how to look, what to eat and how to feel. No wonder most of us grow up with a negative self-esteem!

Desi Williamson goes on to say:

"A child who lives with criticism learns to condemn. On the other hand...a child who lives with encouragement learns to be confident."

If you need more proof of this, you should read *How to Win Friends and Influence People* by Dale Carnegie[3], which clearly states that one way to lose friends is to be that critical friend who always corrects people. No one likes being corrected, so procrastination is thought to be a kind of protection against all those negative comments or feedback that you might get when you do something. If you don't do anything, you won't be judged, therefore a lot of us would rather not do anything.

As children, when our parents withheld praise from us, this meant we always felt that whatever we did was not good enough and that somehow we needed to do more. So we told ourselves, "It could be better if only I gave it more time" so we 'if only' all over ourselves and our tasks and goals – trying to be this person when all we really need to be is ourselves and realise that what we do now is enough until we can do better.

The message this gives us is that there's never a time to rest, we must always keep going – how dare you rest? What have you actually done to deserve a rest? I grew up feeling that I

---

[3] *Carnegie, Dale 2006, How to Win Friends and Influence People., Vermilion Press.*

needed to have permission to take a break so, even when I was resting, I felt like I should be doing something. As an adult and mother, sometimes I'll ask my daughter if it's okay to rest and she will respond, "Mum, why do you always feel guilty about taking a well-deserved break?"

I just have this feeling that I'm a lazy person.

One good thing about being able to manage your time well is that it allows you to be more organised and it means that, for each and every task that you take on, you will have a good idea of how much time it will take. When you're a good time manager, you tend to plan your time well ahead so, for instance, you may have a goal that you want to achieve within three months. Planning well means that you will be able to allocate enough time over that three-month period to allow you to finish the tasks and ensure that you reach that goal.

I am always reminded of this quote by Benjamin Franklin which I first heard from one of my lecturers, "*Failing to plan, is planning to fail.*"

The Benefits of Managing Your Time Effectively:

- You're more organised.
- It reduces stress levels and anxiety because, with the ability to plan ahead, you have more control over your life and spend less time fire-fighting at the last minute.
- People around you will fall in line and appreciate and understand that you don't mess around with your time, so they won't mess around with your time either.

Let's take a look at how effective time management can make a huge difference for those running their own businesses, entrepreneurs, students, those who love to read, those who aspire to write, those who manage others and those who rely on technology in their lives.

CHAPTER ONE

BEING A PRODUCTIVE BUSINESS OWNER

Whether you are an entrepreneur or self-employed, running your own business means that you have to be a very good manager of time. You have no boss and, more than likely, no employees when you first start your own business. Not having a boss is great, something you have probably always dreamed of, and so now it has finally happened – it's bliss and heaven all rolled into one. And, if you work from home, that's even better...you just need to cross the hallway to get to work in the spare bedroom...or just grab your laptop whilst still in bed and just get on with it. But we are not all as self-motivated and on the ball as we would like to be.

"Time management is life management"

Being employed means that you have a job description and some hierarchy that forces you to deliver results, or at least 'appear to work' and to a specific deadline. You can't just wing it. There are meetings with the boss or your colleagues. You have the dreaded one to one sessions with difficult managers or stubborn employees. There are urgent emails with far too many people copied in, so ignoring them simply isn't an option. Like most people, as a dedicated employee you put in more than you are paid for :) Overworked and underpaid is the mantra of the employee.

Are You More Productive?

But hold on, now that you're on your own and you can do what you want, when you want, it actually gets harder to be productive and manage all those wonderful 24 hours that are now yours to do with as you please. The problem is, those hours are passing by and you could easily rack up hours, months, years, decades, even a lifetime of doing nothing or promising to get back to a project that you started and then have multiple projects on the go with not one of them close to completion. If you find yourself in this boat, give yourself a pat on the back, at least it shows that you're not short of an idea or two – you are creative and like to multi-task. However, the downside is that people usually get measured or judged on results and if projects don't get finished, then there are no results. And that is how frustrations kicks in.

Where Are You Going?

Now, go back to the 10 things you listed as having done in the previous 24 hours that I asked you to prepare earlier. Do the tasks or activities you listed take you closer to your goals? If not, this is a great time to develop new tasks that will move you closer to those goals. With each task you undertake, you are either moving closer to or further away from your goals.

To make sure that you become the kind of person who delivers results, you need to change your mindset. One thing that I would definitely recommend when you start your own business is to write a job description for yourself with all the tasks that you need to do and the responsibilities you will have. It doesn't matter if you can't do them all, keep adding to the list. This is great as it serves a dual purpose of identifying what you can do and what needs to be delegated to someone else. Since we work for ourselves, the one area we struggle with the most and which stops us from getting ahead is the ability to delegate.

We often think we are not ready or our operations are not large enough to delegate but, the problem is, most businesses that employ staff do much better and grow much faster than when the boss decides to do it all by themselves. Even if it's just someone to take calls, respond to emails, update the website or social media content – each will be one less thing for you to worry about while you concentrate on growing your business. Don't major in minor things.

Getting Things Done

In his book, *E-Myth Revisited*, Michael Gerber[4] talks about the difference between a doer and a business builder. A business builder – the visionary who has a vision and puts the structure in place – does not get involved in the day-to-day management of the business. He manages the operations and the direction of the business. To do the same, we need an organisation chart and job descriptions – don't worry about the positions being filled yet, that will come later.

In the meantime, to make sure you are productive every day, put your job description in a place where you can see it and have a list of things that you need to do to keep your business ticking over. As I provide services, most of my time is taken

---

[4] *Gerber Michael, 2009. The E-Myth Revisited: Why Most Small Businesses Don't Work and What to Do About It, HarperBus*

up doing one of three things – producing content for my business, marketing the business and making sure my clients are happy.

In my business, I break these tasks into bite size checklists so I can identify which can be done in-house and those that need to be delegated to other professionals better than me and who can do it in a fraction of the time that I can – this saves time and, in business, time is money so this is one asset that you want to manage very well.

MOJO TIPS

Put a job description together for yourself if you're running your own business.

Make sure you have a list of what you plan to do from week to week based on your type of business.

Try to have your work planned ahead of you – don't wing it and at the end of the week always check back to see if you've achieved your goals for that week.

"If I had six hours to chop down a tree, I would spend the first four hours sharpening the axe." – Abraham Lincoln

Make sure you spend at least one day a week working on your business. This could be improving your marketing material, chasing up customer testimonials, reading through your competitors' websites and general reading about what's happening in your industry. If you do all these things, you will be in the top 20% of all businesses because most businesses exist on a wing and a prayer which perhaps often leads to them giving up too soon.

The Time Struggle

If you struggle with time, try this. Use a stopwatch to get you started, set it up before you begin a task, give yourself 20 minutes then begin – you will soon find yourself engrossed in the task. I use this hack to help me with tasks that I would rather not do. Remember, some of us find it difficult to start a task but, once we get into it, it's not that bad. Make sure you try to finish your tasks, break them down if they appear too big.

So, for instance, you want to update your social media profiles – take one of these at a time – let's look at Facebook. Change the picture one day, do the 'about us' area on another day, and so on. Just do one area a day and, by the end of the week, you should have a brand new Facebook page.

It's better than seeing the whole task as ONE thing. Tasks can be made up of mini steps and you can break them up to make it easier for you to start.

CHAPTER TWO

BEING A PRODUCTIVE READER

Well, it's often been said that readers are leaders and one study goes so far as to suggest that if you read over 60 books a year, you will earn six times that which the average reader earns in a year – the average reader reads less than one book a year!

Are You Well Read?

Absolutely woeful – most of what I do and know today comes from my love of reading. I have been reading for longer than I can remember. I used to read the Reader's Digest from the age of seven and by the time I was 10 I was reading James Hadley Chase and Mills and Boons among others – it's where all my pocket money went as a teenager. So, for me, reading has been, and remains, very important in moving me from point A to B.

When I realised that I couldn't read as much as I wanted to because of time pressure, I did some research into reading more quickly and got myself a copy of *Speed Reading* by Tony Buzan[5] and, based on the suggestions in the book, I can now read whole books much faster.

---

[5] *Buzan Tony, 2003. The Speed Reading Book: Read more, learn more. BBC Publishing.*

Moving Targets

For 2020, I set myself a target of 50 books – that equates to one book a week. I'm behind because of other projects but I know that I can do it and in fact I have to because I actually committed to doing this in an email I sent to those on my mailing list. I will be publishing a list of these 50 books when I've finished them – make yourself accountable to others, it's the best way to make sure that you deliver on your goals...think of Weight Watchers. They make the dieters accountable through their weekly weigh-ins which are also tracked on paper or via the app.

"When you fall, if you can look up you can get up." – Les Brown

Are You a Night Owl?

For me, reading is best done at night before I go to bed and I can manage about 100 pages in an hour. I rarely watch TV, I gave this up as part of my 50 before 50 bucket list when, in 2013, I spent the whole summer abroad and had recorded my favourite soaps. When I got back to the UK, there were over 200 hours of recordings that I had to catch up on. Straight away I decided that I couldn't possibly give all that time to TV, so I stopped watching TV altogether. Now my former three hour nightly TV time is spent doing other more productive things. That summer trip cured me of my TV addiction, so now I have more time to read and write.

Now it's your turn. What do you currently do that takes up your time but does not produce the results you want?

What's one productive thing that you could replace this with?

Find a Good Read

Back to reading, decide on the books you want to read. A good start is to aim for a book a month. Go to Google and search for the books in your area of interest and select a few. If your budget is tight, then sign up for a Kindle app, this allows you to buy any book for at least half the price of the paperback, it's stored in your Kindle and you can read it anywhere and anytime on any gadget of your choice.

If you prefer paperback versions of books and you are lucky to have a library near you, then visit it, select a few books and start reading. If you prefer to listen to books, your local library may have some audio books, grab them. You can also sign up to audible or similar platforms for a small monthly subscription and you can listen to books on the gadget of your choice – phone, tablet or laptop. Or, if you like your information in bite sized format, then Podcasts might be your thing. The hosts talk about anything from sports to crime to writing. Whatever your flavour.

CHAPTER THREE

BEING A PRODUCTIVE STUDENT

Most students go to school to learn and have to remember enough to pass exams and produce coherent assignments etc.

My Experience

When I went to secondary school, we weren't taught how to study strategically so by the time I reached university I was like everyone else, swotting for as many hours as possible. Back then, we called it "the graveyard shift" where you would study from 10 pm until about 4 am, tucked away in the dining hall or classroom, and only return to the dormitory in the morning for a few hours of sleep. That was like a badge of honour. You had this air of self-importance about you, and the other students would look at you as if your first class results were a guarantee. Total rubbish! This is a formula that I used all through my university education - studying for up to 18 hours a day. I would go to the library at 9 am, leave when it closed at 9 pm, get home, eat and then do another two hours before collapsing in a heap and waking up the next day only to do the same thing all over again.

Studying with Other Commitments

Fast forward a few years to when I had children and wanted to study for my professional accountancy exams. I realised that my approach to studying at university was now no longer sustainable. I had a full-time job and two children under seven, so there weren't enough hours in the day to achieve everything. Thus I had to find a better way, so I turned to the internet. This was in the early 2000s – yes, I'm an early adopter, I found Tony Buzan who was then talking about how to study effectively (he also wrote about speed reading, if you remember) so I bought his book and, as I began to read, overnight it transformed the way I studied!

In his book, *Use Your Memory*, Tony Buzan[6] explains that the human brain can only concentrate from between 30 to 50 minutes at a time and that one must take a break after that time to keep learning at its peak. He also talked about recall, and you will agree with me that this is the most important part of studying. Recall is easier if the study periods are planned, shorter and with adequate breaks.

I went from studying 18 hours a day to just four and I was getting much better results. This is something that I have used with my children too, so I know it works. My son achieved a first class degree in mechanical engineering and my daughter got the second best GCSEs in her school and was even featured in our local paper. And I passed my final accountancy exams (ACCA) – four of the most challenging and toughest papers ever set (I think!) and sat (I know!) – first time, no re-sits or referrals. I'm not a genius – I have failed exams like no other – I failed my first GSCE exams – and one of them was

---

[6] *Buzan Tony, 2003. Use Your Memory, BBC Publishing.*

English :). I also spent four years doing a BTEC course which should have taken two years so I have had serious failures and I tell people that, while I don't have a Mensa[7] brain, I do have an intelligent strategy that is teachable and can be used by any average student to achieve above average results.

Powerful Techniques that I Have Mastered

To break it down, what Tony Buzan did was to study the human brain. He found out that, when studying, the most important part of that process was how much you could recall after studying – what did you remember after a study period? – so you had to test yourself after each one. He also found that the brain cannot concentrate for more than two hours at a time and even those two-hour periods require short 10-15-minute breaks. So, studying for 18 hours on the trot is a waste of time and the return on investment (ROI) of that time is very poor.

Armed with this new knowledge, I cut down my studying time to two hours in the morning and two in the evening, and to make my studying even faster and more productive, I rarely used the prescribed textbooks to revise. I spent my time using the shorter revision books, which contained just questions and answers on the subject. I would only refer to my study text if an area was not clear enough and the results speak for themselves – I have never failed an exam since.

"Discipline is the bridge between goals and accomplishment." – Jim Rohn

---

[7] https://www.mensa.org.uk/iq-tests

Mind Map Your Knowledge

The book also introduced me to mind mapping, which is a pictorial or graphical representation that can be used to condense notes, generate new ideas, brainstorm, team build, in fact to plan almost anything. It helps to clarify and generate new ideas, and I used this to analyse my study texts into manageable bits. At my peak, when studying for exams, I could mind map an entire book on one page! Using keywords and images! It requires lots of different coloured pens and you soon become a Picasso, Van Gogh or Da Vinci! I actually mind map all my training courses and lectures.

Planning Ahead

When my children were young, to make my studying more effective, I designed a timetable. I used lots of mind maps and did two hours in the morning dividing my time up so that I read for the first hour, took a 15–20 minute break and then did the second hour. It was not only more productive, but I felt happier knowing I only had to dedicate 2-2½ hours to studying and I usually did two sessions, one in the morning and one in the evening. It was great, and I passed my exams.

A year later, I followed the same system and passed my final exams – first time passes, with a full-time job, two kids under nine and with only a week off work, and I succeeded.

It does work and, despite having had great success with it myself, surprisingly none of my friends have bought the book even though I know some of them are struggling to pass exams.

CHAPTER FOUR

BEING A PRODUCTIVE WRITER

Well, I am an authority in this area since, while I have read many books on how to write consistently, I have instead procrastinated consistently, putting time aside to write but then finding myself doing other things instead.

My Writing Woes

This book should have been out long before now. However, an exciting opportunity for me to become a lecturer came up and I couldn't say no. This now takes up quite a bit of my time as I am continually researching and regularly developing new course materials. I do a lot of other things consistently, but writing is the one thing that I still need to do more of. Last night I read about the most prolific writers – one has written over a million books, albeit by a machine. The only other person who comes close is someone[8] who has written 904 books the traditional way – that is a milestone – that's a book a week for nearly 18 years!

Wow...to achieve this, first you have to consider what to write about – how do you know if you're not repeating yourself?!

---

[8] https://en.wikipedia.org/wiki/Kathleen_Lindsay

Big Bodacious Goal...I just want to write seven books – that seems to be the magic number to make a good income consistently...if you write a good book, people want to read more from you and if you only have one book out then you are leaving money on the table as it were...

So, as a writer, let's plan to write that blockbuster, bestseller or award-winning book – or even one that's enjoyable would be great!

Question Yourself

What questions do you need to ask yourself? First, what do you want to write about – and why do you want to write? These are very important questions and will give you valuable insight – the WHY you want to write. What's your reason? To leave a legacy? To write your own or someone else's story in order to inspire? Or simply because you are just gifted and like to tell a good story?

MOJO TIPS

Whatever the reason, take a few minutes to write at least five sentences about why you want to write, then summarise those into just one sentence. Go one step further, print that sentence using a great font and perhaps add a picture to it, frame it and put it where you can see it every day. This will remind and motivate you to take action.

Writing Prompts to Get You Started:

- You wake up one morning, grab your passport and head to the airport and ask for a ticket for the next flight out. Where do you end up and what happens? Who do you meet?

- You have just been told that you were born a twin. You are about to meet this twin for the first time tomorrow. What do you ask them? How would you prepare for the meeting? What would you expect them to look like?

- You have just been selected to go on your favourite reality TV show. Which one would it be and, if you had to choose six celebrities to be on the show with you, who would they be and why?

- You have been asked to write the storyline for the next episode of your favourite TV programme. Prepare the outline of it.

- Take a bus from the beginning to the end of its journey. Write about what you see.

The hugely inspiring writer's book by Dorothea Brande, *Becoming a Writer*[9], is great for those writers who keep procrastinating. My favourite quote from the book is:

"If you can't write, then give it up and find something else to do"

She is right because, if you can't get into the habit of writing, you will not write that book. She advocates two things that will help you. First, you must have a 'why' and then you must adopt a writing schedule. For me, I schedule my writing time twice a week and I get up early to do an hour each time.

---

[9] *Brande Dorothea, 1981. Becoming a Writer, Jeremy P Tarcher.*

The Dreaded Writer's Block

The problem here is that you are bringing your analytical friend along on your writing journey – leave him behind, he'll kill your dreams before they are even hatched – and there they will remain in the holding bay, waiting to be birthed by you but never getting a chance because of that critical friend on your shoulder – that part of you that believes it knows everything – even the response of others, that your story is not unique, blah blah. You need to tell that friend to take a break while you get down to writing...

As I often say, if the bible can be translated into so many different languages and still make sense, what is your issue with grammar and language? No matter what you have written, it can be made into something that makes sense...Get the first rubbish down – I have never met an editor who can edit an empty page – for an editor to do their work, you must write something. Give yourself a break, get the first draft out and your writing will get better.

Try Dorothea Brande's morning pages idea – just get up every morning and write three pages about anything at all – whatever is on your mind – just write, even if it means writing, "I have nothing to say or write and I have to fill these pages and so I am going to even if I am going to write rubbish"...yes you can write rubbish or write something better, that's okay. Just remember this, the greatest writers, the most talented writers of our time are in the graveyard – they took their incredible talents and award-winning books with them to the grave. Please do not deny the world the pleasure of your own writing – let us celebrate you, read you, be inspired, moved and have you touch our lives.

For a few prompts for your morning pages, try answering these questions:

Who do you hate and why?

What do you love and why?

What has happened to you that you wish hadn't?

What hasn't happened to you that you wish would happen?

If the idea of three morning pages isn’t for you, aim to write at particular times every day instead. Make sure you pick a time and put it in your diary – a digital diary with a reminder, even if it’s only 10 minutes a day. That's an hour a week more than you’re writing now.

CHAPTER FIVE

BEING A PRODUCTIVE MANAGER

Some of us manage other people and time management for us is crucial because, if we don't manage how we take responsibility for our team's problems, we might find ourselves managing their workload as well as our own workload and this will take up even more of our time.

Whose Monkeys Are You Carrying?

In *The One Minute Manager*, the author Ken Blanchard[10] explains the importance of delegation and responsibility by using monkeys as an analogy. These 'monkeys' are identified as a problem or a work in progress so, for example, one of your staff members comes to you and says something like "I can't do this" or "I'm trying to find this...." and you think you want to be supportive as a manager so you offer to help and say, "Don't worry I'll sort that out". Guess what? You've just taken the monkey off their back and you've put it on your own back. That's just one issue, but can you imagine if you are managing a team of 10 and you take one issue/problem from each of them? By offering to help them solve their problems, that's 10 more tasks on top of your own workload.

---

[10] *Blanchard Ken et al, 2004 The One Minute Manager, Harper Collins.*

Before they came to see you about this problem, the monkey was actually on their back. The moment you stop what you are doing and start to listen to the problem, one leg of that monkey is now on your back. When you then accept and say things like "I'll look into that" or "Leave it with me", the monkey is firmly on your back and guess what? You'll be the one running around and you've just changed positions because your staff member is now going to manage you. Yes, what's happened is that you've reversed positions and now you'll have to give an update to that staff member!

So, be careful with your staff members and what you take on because you need to do your own job and your own job is to manage them.

One solution offered in the book is that, when anybody comes to you with a problem, help them to analyse it and then get their commitment to what they need to do next. Make sure the problem is allocated to a person so if it's not the actual person with the problem, find somebody else to do it but make sure you can always locate who is dealing with the problem to track its progress.

If someone comes to you with a problem and tells you they don't know the answer, tell them that you don't know the answer either and you don't think that the company can afford to employ people who don't have answers. But where does that leave you? Instead try this:

If someone does come to you with a problem, you will probably know their situation. Maybe they know what to do but don't realise it. Maybe they know enough but are being lazy. Or perhaps they truly don't know because the situation is new for them. Here's a great opportunity to coach them.

Asking the person questions that are clearly relevant to the issue - such as where, when, how and what - is a good starting point. Add some 'silence' (thinking time). This allows the person to mine their own knowledge and find ways to identify solutions to their problems.

Delegating well and getting those that you are line managing to think about how they can come up with solutions will empower them and also keep the company running efficiently and effectively.

CHAPTER SIX

USING TECHNOLOGY FOR PRODUCTIVITY

Well, this is quite a large subject because we all now use some form of technology to produce our work or which is supposed to make our lives more productive.

Effective Technology

Technology can make you more effective and I do use technology to save time. For instance, I started paying most bills online as soon as it became possible to do so over 15 years ago. I'm sure most of you do this now.

Shopping online also means you can save more time, with fewer trips to the shops for groceries and clothes. I've been shopping online now for a long time. I like technology and new things, so I started shopping on Amazon in 2002 and started grocery shopping soon after. This saves me a lot of time and I'm able to do other things rather than spend it on the high street, shopping.

One other area that technology helps me in is productivity in my work, and that meant eventually getting the holy trinity of Apple products. I had a MacBook and an iPad, but my phone had always been an android. A couple of years ago I was looking to get a new phone, and I decided to get an iPhone. The major reason I chose an iPhone is because with all the other android phones, I had found it difficult to sync the information over all my gadgets. I'd put a date in my Samsung which I'd forget to transfer to my iPad and then I'd miss the appointment; and having to do backups took so long.

Alexa, Are You There?

Last year I used Google to transcribe my journals online so this could be a suitable alternative for you too. I'm able to type up to 1700 words in 45 minutes. With dictation, I get 2,250 words in 45 minutes, so that means I get more than an extra 500 words in the same time. Very effective and a better use of my time.

To write this book, I used 'Siri' – dictating my book onto my phone via the notes app. These notes also appeared on my Mac when I got onto my laptop, so all I needed to do was copy and paste my notes into my Scrivener – this saved at least half of my normal writing time.

The Holy Grail of Writers

Scrivener is software that I have always raved about. It's what I use to write my books and my blogs too. I am also writing this book as part of the Nanowrimo, a yearly competition that challenges writers to write 50,000 words over 30 days in the month of November. Today is the 25th, so it looks like I will achieve this because I'm dictating my words. This means I can hold my phone and talk to it in any quiet place, so this is a test and I'll see how well it works. This will be in draft mode, and because I'm speaking, I know the accuracy is going to be poorer than if I had typed it out. However, it will save me time because we speak a lot faster than we type and, for me, when I have a thought it's good if I can just get it down without having to use the keyboard because sometimes that makes the process slower and I lose some ideas that way.

After much resistance to getting any social media apps on my phone, I finally got my top three – Facebook, Instagram and LinkedIn; however, I switch off notifications just to make sure I'm not continually interrupted during my day.

Another way I use technology to make my work more effective is by sending bulk messages so, if I want to send a message to a certain group of people, I'll do that either by putting the recipients into a group or on a mailing list and I have found WhatsApp to be a great tool for this. Then obviously for meetings, instead of taking time to travel to see people even if you're both in the same city, it actually makes sense to use Skype or FaceTime. After all, you speak to people abroad using the system so it should be able to work for us even if we're in the same city.

"Our meetings are held to discuss many problems which would never arise if we held fewer meetings." – Ashleigh Brilliant

Train with Tech

I have used Skype technology to train and coach clients and I find this works better because there's no need to travel and it's actually more engaging, so there's less likelihood of being distracted. The clients are more focused because of the need to look at the screen if you're showing them material and you can actually see them learning. I think this is an effective way to engage with people. We also all know many people who do webinars so, instead of searching for a location to attend a course, we can actually do it online – you can deliver one or you can attend one. All this means technology really has changed our approach to learning, working and running a business. More recently, I have used other online tools to teach such as Zoom and MS Teams and the lesser known BigBlueButton.

One online digital event management service that I'm sure you're probably aware of is Eventbrite. Now, if you've run any kind of event you know how much effort and stress this involves but what Eventbrite allows you to do is to list details of the event on their platform so when you post it, either with flyers or online, using online social media to promote it, people can book directly via Eventbrite, freeing you from needless administration. You can also use it as a guest list and tick attendees off it as they respond.

I decided to put my first book, *Unleash Your Business MOJO!*[11], on Amazon because, as we all know, many people now prefer to carry books on their phones. I can't take my books everywhere with me. I do a lot of speaking engagements and training, and I want the people I meet to be able to buy the book without me getting involved in that supply chain. Welcome Amazon – I offer the paperback, the e-book and the audible versions so, if people want to buy the book, they can go straight there and buy it, an excellent example of ecommerce on a very micro level.

When I was organising the book launch, I realised that many people may not have cash on them but most will have a card,

---

[11] *Obadina M, 2016 Unleash Your Business MOJO!, Mo's MOJO.*

so I signed up for a payment system that allowed people to pay using their cards. I chose iZettel and this has proven to be very useful for my business.

Online storage is another big time saver so I use cloud facilities such as One Drive and Google Drive just to make sure that I have access to my files wherever I go, thus reducing the need for a USB and the dangers that come with that.

Based on our use of digital media, my business consultancy was shortlisted for the Chambers Award in 2017, and I also train and support businesses to automate their business processes.

CHAPTER SEVEN

THE PURSUIT OF GOALS

Goals, Values and Self-esteem

Turning to goal setting, when your goals are clear, decisions are easy to make. Do you realise that hesitation could be a sign that you are not sufficiently focused or are perhaps not pursuing the right goals?

What *Really* Matters to You?

This could be because your goals don't align with your values and skill set. Look at the list of values below, it's not exhaustive and you might want to add some of your own once you've checked your goals and the values they entail.

Abundance	Acceptance	Accessibility
Accomplishment	Accountability	Accuracy
Achievement	Acknowledgement	Activeness
Advancement	Adventure	Affection
Affluence	Aggressiveness	Agility

Alertness	Altruism	Amazement
Ambition	Amusement	Anticipation
Appreciation	Approachability	Approval
Art	Articulacy	Artistry
Assertiveness	Assurance	Attentiveness
Attractiveness	Audacity	Availability
Awareness	Awe	Balance
Calmness	Camaraderie	Candour
Capability	Care	Carefulness
Celebrity	Certainty	Challenge
Change	Charity	Charm
Confidence	Conformity	Congruency
Dependability	Depth	Desire
Determination	Devotion	Devoutness
Dexterity	Dignity	Diligence
Enjoyment	Entertainment	Enthusiasm
Environmentalism	Ethics	Euphoria

Excellence	Excitement	Exhilaration
Expectancy	Expediency	Experience
Family	Fascination	Fashion
Fearlessness	Ferocity	Friendship
Frugality	Fun	Gallantry
Generosity	Gentility	Giving
Grace	Gratitude	Gregariousness
Growth	Guidance	Happiness
Harmony	Health	Heart
Helpfulness	Heroism	Holiness
Honesty	Hopefulness	Hospitality
Humility	Humour	Hygiene
Intrepidness	Introspection	Introversion
Intuition	Intuitiveness	Inventiveness
Investing	Involvement	Joy
Judiciousness	Justice	Keenness
Kindness	Knowledge	Leadership

Learning	Liberation	Liberty
Lightness	Liveliness	Logic
Longevity	Love	Loyalty
Majesty	Marriage	Mastery
Maturity	Meaning	Order
Organisation	Originality	Outdoors
Outlandishness	Outrageousness	Partnership
Patience	Passion	Peace
Perceptiveness	Perfection	Perkiness
Perseverance	Persistence	Persuasiveness
Philanthropy	Piety	Playfulness
Pleasantness	Pleasure	Poise
Polish	Popularity	Potency
Power	Practicality	Pragmatism
Precision	Preparedness	Presence
Pride	Privacy	Proactivity
Professionalism	Prosperity	Prudence

Punctuality	Purity	Rationality
Realism	Reason	Responsibility
Rest	Restraint	Reverence
Richness	Rigour	Sacredness
Sacrifice	Sagacity	Tranquillity
Truth	Unshakeability	Wisdom

Which values resonate with you the most? Pick the top 10. These should be at the forefront of what you do. If your career or business does not allow you to use and develop these values, then you may need to look for ways to include the values that are important to you or pivot into a role or hobby that allows you to use them.

Going Back to Our Roots

However, the best personal value and the greatest gift that you need in life is given to you by the age of seven and that is self-esteem. If you haven't got it by then, you had better start working towards getting it – with no self-esteem you will struggle to achieve most of your goals. If you need to, you might have to pretend to have self-esteem because otherwise it will be difficult to set goals and to achieve them. You will read books, go on courses, listen to motivational talks, watch YouTube videos, but take NO ACTION.

"Until one is committed, there is hesitancy, the chance to draw back, always ineffectiveness." – William Hutchison Murray

I used to suffer from self-esteem issues in some areas and this held me back because I felt that I wasn't good enough, didn't look the part etc. but I realised that this was just a story and there were very few facts to back it up. It stemmed from low self-esteem. For example, I used to have a great fear of public speaking and opted out of any task that would require me to face an audience. Then I decided to improve this by joining Toastmasters[12], this changed my life and I now get paid to speak.

Goals – Committing to Paper

One very important thing for you to do is to take a few of your main goals and write those down. This is one key part of achieving goals, and there's something magical that happens when your goals are written down as opposed to just keeping them in your head. The mind is terrible at organising and remembering what you want to do and research shows that, when you write your goals down, you are more likely to achieve them.

"Remember, you cannot hit a target that you cannot see"

In her study, Dr. Gail Matthews,[13] a psychology professor at the Dominican University in California, discovered that those

---

[12] https://www.toastmasters.org/

[13] https://scholar.dominican.edu/cgi/viewcontent.cgi?article=1265&context=news-releases

who wrote down their goals and dreams on a regular basis achieved those desires at a significantly higher level than those who did not. She found that you become 42% more likely to achieve your goals and dreams simply by writing them down on a regular basis.

MOJO TIPS

Goal Setting – Some Helpful Tips

So, once you've committed your goals to paper, how are you going to set about achieving them? Here are a few tips:

List the benefits of achieving the goal

Plan the goal – break it down into five sub goals/steps

Record your progress – good or bad

Reward yourself when you hit a milestone

Be accountable to others – coach/public accountability/on social media

This last point is important. If it helps, PAY people to hold you accountable. Get a coach – it's called PAIN money. If you're paying someone to whom you have to explain why you didn't do the things that you said you were going to do, you're more likely to do them – trust me on this one. It's the same way that Usain Bolt, Serena Williams and Tiger Woods and most world-class athletes are able to consistently deliver better results than they could have done alone. I've used this strategy myself and most of my clients benefit from this service as they see their ideas take shape quickly – instead of just day dreaming about taking action, they are motivated to take action.

All the tips are particularly important to accomplishing a major goal because you can break it down into achievable tasks or sub goals. Examples of major goals could include:

Starting a business

Writing a book

Getting a new job

Studying for exams

Before you start on the small tasks and sub goals, smarten up the actual major goal.

For example, if you want to start your business in December 2021, then divide this milestone up into smaller steps with dates attached, which could look like this:

January: I will become clear about my vision and mission

February: I will research my industry and competitors to look for trends

March: I will do some research into my target audience

April: I will send out questionnaires to my target audience to crystallise my product/service offerings

May: I will work on my branding, business name, colours and website etc.

Align Your Goals to Rewards

Time management needs focus because, without focus, it's difficult to achieve. When you're thinking about managing your time, it's important to choose goals based on your vision and which align with your values, something that you are working towards. This makes it easier for you to stay on track as these goals will motivate you to get started and it means that you will be able to get more done.

For example, if you're thinking of taking a break in six months' time, which could be a holiday abroad and you are also thinking about writing a book, why not link the two so then the holiday or break becomes a gift or reward for attempting to write the book. Six months is a good length of time to get the outline of the book ready or perhaps develop the chapters if that's how you write.

"The bad news is time flies. The good news is you're the pilot." – Michael Altshuler

The start could be just that maybe you want to do some research about what it takes to write a book if you've never written one before. Your first step could be going on a writing course, just take one step and try to do something that will move you closer to your goal of writing a book. You will feel better and you can build on that motivation to keep you going forward. Knowing that it's tied up with a holiday, which is something fun, should help to move you forward.

The same would apply if you're planning to learn a new language or lose weight, whatever the goal is, try to link it to something exciting and fun that encourages you to go with that goal.

If it's a longer term goal, that's even better. You might have decided that once you hit 50 you want to retire and you're 40 now, so you've got 10 years in which to achieve that goal or vision. What you need to do is break it down and think about what you can do now that can help you to achieve that goal. It could be that you need a better job that pays more, but to get a better job you need to acquire more skills which might mean you need to go on a short course.

So think about what you can do now to make sure your goal happens. Could it be that you need to ask for a promotion, or start to look for things that you can do to increase your income so that you can retire earlier? Like those things that could also be a hobby, something you've been thinking of doing but not quite got yourself round to doing.

Smarten up Your Goals

Remember, when you set your goals you really need to stretch your boundaries, get out of your comfort zone. Staying in the same place is the same thing as going backwards, you need to be heading forwards, your goals need to be moving targets, not set. Your goals must be SMART – you must measure them so you know that they're Specific, Measurable, Achievable, Realistic and Time framed.

"Lack of direction, not lack of time, is the problem. We all have twenty-four hour days." – Zig Ziglar

You need the time frames but, if they're not easily measurable, it's hard to track your progress. You could decide you want to be a better business person but how will you know that you have become a better business person? Is it when you win that particular award that you've had your eyes on?

The key is to find something that you can link the goal to. It doesn't always need to be measurable, but it needs to have an action which, when it happens, acknowledges that you have achieved your goal (meeting someone like a mentor/respected person/being invited to do a TEDx talk) or something else – perhaps when you've published that book or you're called to speak at a particular event. These could be ways for you to measure success.

Just make sure the goal is tied up to what you really want to do or what you enjoy doing – your passion – because it's going to be difficult to set goals round things you don't really enjoy doing and I use myself as an example of this. When I started my first business in accounting, I did all the work and found that I didn't like the book-keeping aspect of it. I didn't like this at all and found it boring, and repetitive. I changed this around by teaming up with someone who actually liked doing book-keeping while I did other tasks that I enjoyed more like dealing directly with business processes and marketing.

I now work in business management and support. I can see that this is exactly where my passion lies because looking at the traction I've been able to make over the last three to four years, the momentum has been crazy. I've won awards, I've delivered various training programmes, I've added new programmes and new services. And now, based on my expertise, I have added lecturing to what I do. It's great to get the opportunity to share my knowledge and experience with budding and future entrepreneurs, and I just love it.

Now, when you're setting your own goals and you're thinking about the future, this could be based on something that gives you a positive feeling, maybe from an experience in your life or it could be something that you enjoy doing so much that it makes you come alive!

Treat Yourself

Rewards help to motivate us or make us feel better. Next time you hit a milestone in reaching your goal, do something great; or even if you are feeling down, don't go for the usual solution – clothes shopping, buying food, etc. Treat yourself to an experience instead. In his book, *59 Seconds*, Richard Wiseman[14] dedicates a chapter to his findings on what makes people happy for longer. His research shows that, while a new car or a new gadget might keep us happy in the short term, experiences keep us happy for much longer. So, next time you want to treat yourself, try taking on a new hobby, meeting new people, visiting a museum, trying a new restaurant or taking a mini break.

MOJO TIPS

So, thinking about a reward, what have you always wanted to do but never seem to have the time to achieve? Schedule some time for a fresh experience or a tangible treat, whatever works...

Hobbies

Joining a club

Meeting new people

[14] *Wiseman Richard. 2015, 59 Seconds: Think a Little, Change a Lot. Pan; Main Market edition.*

Learning a new skill

New sport

Losing weight

Momentary happiness

New home

Pay rise

New car

New gadget

CHAPTER EIGHT

BEAT PROCRASTINATION

Research suggests that nearly 25%[15] of people identify procrastination as a problem when trying to achieve their goals. However, we have to take into account that this does not begin to highlight the scale of the problem – given that this result is based on those who could be bothered to return the questionnaire within the specified time."

So, let's examine those bad habits - indecision and procrastination, the two siblings that hold you back...and cause havoc when they come along and interfere with your goals.

False Rewards, Missed Opportunities and Fear

Procrastination is a learned evolutionary habit that used to protect us from actual threats. It was necessary for survival when we lived in the wild. Those threats are no longer there, but we still believe they are real and we're great at finding avoidance techniques to stop us from doing what we must do. You have a 'to do list' yet you go into the kitchen and make yourself a cup of tea or, in my case, bake a cake!

[15] https://onlinelibrary.wiley.com/doi/abs/10.1111/ijsa.12048

I could find myself on YouTube on a Saturday night, watching my favourite sewing and DIY tutorials, sometimes finding myself skipping from video to video, landing on a completely different and unrelated one and then when I read the comments section, I can see that when other viewers started their internet journey, this was not the video they set out to watch either. They were probably just on Facebook or Instagram, where most of our online journeys begin these days, then we see something. It could be a friend's comment or a video and you just click click – clicking away our future, clicking away from our goals and clicking further away from the life we deserve.

"Be like a postage stamp – stick to one thing until you get there." – Josh Billings

So, we've looked at rewarding ourselves when we've achieved something. Now let's look at some ways our procrastination is rewarded.

Well, this actually does happen. Sometimes when you've spotted something you want, whether in a favourite shop or an online store, the price then either drops or the item goes on sale. This could also relate to airline tickets or even house prices.

Suffering from Imposter Syndrome?

Your mind tells you that you've just been rewarded for waiting and that procrastinating can actually give you what you want. Obviously, this is not consistently correct because, the truth is, we can also lose opportunities because of our procrastination.

Sometimes those opportunities are missed because we think that maybe we're not qualified enough or that we need to get more information or do more research, and then maybe we would be in a better position to start or take advantage of an opportunity. This is what we tell ourselves while we miss out on opportunities, even those that land in our laps.

Richard Branson once said "*If you are given a task, always say yes and then go and find out how to do it, never say no*" because if you're asked to do something, chances are that whoever is asking knows that you are capable of handling it well. So, borrow some of that confidence they have in you and use it to get started.

There are many reasons for procrastination, and some of these include:

- The fear of not being able to control the situation
- The fear of failure or the fear of not been able to complete the task
- And an unusual one, the fear of success

So people think, "What if I do that and become successful? What next?" – does that mean there will be even more work or demands made of me? What if I fail in these? And, for those reasons, they hesitate and don't bother doing it at all.

Worrying About Worrying

"About 91% of our worries do not come true,"

A study by LaFreniere and Newman (2019)[16] proved that most of our worries and fears are unfounded. They found that only 9% of our worries actually happen and, for the two-thirds of those worries that did come true, we could deal with them.

The study further revealed the cost of worry – it takes up a quarter of our daily thinking time. Do you really want to spend that much time thinking when you either can do little about it or are aware that precious time is whittling away?

The Pomodoro Method[17]

The real issue though is that any one of these worries or fears could be squashed simply by seeing it differently, by just spending enough time getting started and tackling it. There are so many different ways to kick start taking action. For example, there is the "Pomodoro Method" where you set the timer for 25 minutes and start a task. Once the timer ends, you take a 5 minute break. Then, if you need to, you just re-start the timer again for another 25 minutes. After every four sets of 25 minutes, you then take a longer break of up to 30 minutes. Eventually you find yourself getting into it, so it turns out most of the fear was false expectations appearing to be real.

Real fear happens if you were to be confronted by a lion whilst walking down the road or if a fire started in your house. It's reacting to actual physical danger. But most of our fears are just future oriented and are what we think may happen. In

---

[16] https://pubmed.ncbi.nlm.nih.gov/31362145/

[17] *https://en.wikipedia.org/wiki/Pomodoro_Technique*

reality, our 'fears' are the anxiety we attach/give to a specific thing or event (Horwitiz, 2013).

Another reason we procrastinate is because we fear that our first attempt at a new task won't be perfect. We believe our first attempt should be award-winning, should be error free, a touch of genius. Scrap that. In the real world, that doesn't happen.

And just to prove this point, at Harvard there is a special section of the library where they keep draft manuscripts of successful and celebrated award-winning authors. They keep these drafts and rough notes so that students can see that the masterpieces didn't happen after one draft, it took several drafts and, having written a book myself, I can testify to that.

Can You Achieve Perfection?

It takes several drafts and re-drafts and when I teach about writing; I tell my students to get that first draft – that rubbish – spat out because until you produce that rubbish draft, the great one won't come out. Writing is like polishing a dirty shoe or a rough diamond – polishing, i.e. writing and getting better at it, will produce better work over time.

Your initial work might be a collection of rubbish, but from that rubbish will come your ideas. It is a process that you must go through to produce your best work, so that's the reason why you shouldn't let worry allow you to procrastinate. If you're anticipating brilliance at your first attempt, let me allay your fears and release you from that burden because I can guarantee 99% of the time it probably won't be a great work of art, it won't be a masterpiece and it won't be award-winning. What it will be is the beginning of that journey towards any or all of those achievements. It can happen. Just remember, you'll get better at anything if you just keep on practicing consistently and stop worrying about it not being perfect from the outset.

Procrastination: Deal with It Now, Don't Give in to It!

So how do you identify and deal with procrastination?

Procrastination can be best understood when compared to motivation. Motivation is the ability to get things done whilst procrastination is the opposite because it means that you are not doing the tasks you should be doing at the right time. You are postponing them to a later date. The problem with this is that you will suffer twice. Being aware of the task you should be doing occupies space in your mind, causing you stress, and then procrastinating also causes you to lose out on potential opportunities.

Piers Steel[18] carried out some research into procrastination and found that the main reason we procrastinate is because we don't feel that we would enjoy or be successful at doing the tasks, and we also believe that the reward is too far away. We want instant gratification, which is an evolutionary trait that no longer serves us well. In current times, we have to plan ahead.

So, how about some ways to deal with procrastination and get things done:

---

[18] https://psycnet.apa.org/doiLanding?doi=10.1037%2F0033-2909.133.1.65

1. Break your tasks or goals into mini steps. This makes each task manageable and, because they are so small, there is a greater sense of being able to complete the mini step.
2. Get started using various prompts, like the Pomodoro method I described earlier. Research shows that although we may struggle to get started, once we do, 80% of us are more likely to complete our tasks.
3. Remove distractions from your environment. That could be the TV, your phone, people and other things that distract you from your tasks. A report by Atlassian found that on average we are interrupted 56 times a day – via meetings, social media and our colleagues.
4. Use Parkinson's Law which means that work invariably expands to fill the time we have available even when it could have taken less time, for example, making a 20 minute task last the whole day. To avoid this, set yourself some artificial deadlines so that you can be more productive.
5. Accountability - be accountable in a variety of different ways - use someone else, a group or even join a challenge such as a 30 day writing challenge or 30 day walking challenge.

Time to Reflect

Hopefully, by now you've learnt some new ways to recognise and deal with that bad habit of overthinking things or doing things you're not supposed to be doing rather than getting on with the task at hand.

"The best time to start was last year. Failing that, today will do." – Chris Guillebeau

You understand now why you might choose to tidy your desk, do more research, or make more time to think about something before you actually do it. Or, even worse, why you decide that you want to start tomorrow because you believe you'll wake up early and hit the ground running.

When you get into that kind of frame of mind, it's the result of old patterns and old habits that you need to unlearn to break free of them because, as you know, "If you keep on doing the same things you will keep on getting the same results". You need to have a plan of attack so that when you find yourself not wanting to take action (procrastinating), you can step back a little and really begin to think about the things you say to yourself.

The Burning Questions

"What can I see ahead of me?", "It's going to be so hard to start or complete", "I don't know enough to start now", "Why did I decide to take on this task?". Instead of cementing your doubt by asking these questions, take the power back. Don't act as if you're being told or asked to do it, act like you're taking control, "I choose to do this..." and believe me you can do it because you will have achieved such things before over and over again. Remember, if you have done this task or similar in the past and you have been successful then you have the ability to do it and therefore you definitely can succeed with the task or project ahead of you. It is your mindset at the beginning of a new task that will determine the outcome. "*If you think you can, you will, if you think you can't then you won't*".

People who are successful have also failed, but they have decided that the failure was simply a temporary setback rather than a permanent one. It's an experience to learn from that mistake and try not to repeat it in the future. Everything is an opportunity to learn something. Some successful people see failure as feedback. And you might have heard the saying – *"Don't worry about failures, worry about the chances you miss when you don't even try"*.

Goals Don't Have a Straight Path

Successful people have resilience and have learnt to be able to just keep getting back up, no matter what. There is a chance you won't get it right, there is a chance you might become a laughing stock for a while but you have to ask yourself these questions, is this one thing that I got wrong going to define me? Is that how I want to be remembered? As the person who failed and gave up?

Think about that for a minute. Some things may happen that you might not have control over, so you just have to accept them and take corrective action, perhaps find another way of dealing with it. For example, during the summer I walk 10k steps a day but when the weather changes to winter - cold and dark outside - I dance my steps indoors listening to music. In other words, always look for the alternative approach you can take or try to look ahead at what you can do to change what's happened or what may be about to happen. Look beyond what's happening now.

According to Richard M. Devos[19], the only thing that stands between what you have and what you want in life is the ability to try, and the faith to believe that it's possible.

The Costs of Delays

Procrastination is not just about having a task you're supposed to do and not doing it. It's also about diets that you've promised yourself you would start but never did, it's about that gym membership you pay for every month but never go, it's that online course that you signed up for but never started. It's those books that you bought but never got round to reading, that phone call, that visit that you were supposed to make but never managed.

And sometimes without knowing it, those phone calls could be the last, those visits could be the last. This happened to me with a dear friend. It could be a doctor's appointment that you should have attended, but you kept putting off until things got worse; the bank statement that you should have looked at but kept putting off until the summons that dropped through the letterbox demanded your attention. To avoid constant firefighting, you must avoid being reactive and concentrate on being proactive – setting goals and taking action. Remember that old saying, 'A stitch in time saves nine'? Well, it rings true!

If you do a lot of firefighting in your life, it's because you have failed to plan. You failed to plan, so now the plan is working on you. "Deep" as my daughter would say.

---

[19] Richard M. DeVos, co-founder of Amway, (March 4, 1926 – September 6, 2018) was an American billionaire businessman.

CHAPTER NINE

DITCH THE DISTRACTIONS

What I tend to do when I am working on a task and feel a distraction is to write down exactly what the distractions are. Say I want to listen to a radio programme or Google something random, I'll note that down just to get it out of my head then do what I need to do and go back to that distraction when I take my next break.

Focus on One Thing

Another thing that I've been doing lately is to try to give myself two hours of concentration in any one sitting, aiming to do two of these sessions each day, and this has been working quite well for me.

To some of you, that might not seem like a lot, but for someone who has wasted away hours upon hours of not actually doing anything because they're worried about whether they have the necessary skills or that the outcome may not be satisfactory, this is a significant improvement. Let's put this into the context of worrying and rewards, factors we've already looked at.

For a long time, I spent too much time worrying about the future or how to approach certain goals (not tasks, as we know goals need to be broken down into tasks) and that caused me to waste stupendous amounts of time. I turned it around so you can too. So now, as I said, I just knuckle down and do two sessions of two hours each.

Pareto's Law:

This law is based on the principle that only 20% of our activities produce 80% of our results, hence to be more productive we should focus on the vital 20% of activity. The first step will be to identify those activities that make up the vital 80% of the results.

This exercise is very important, as each of our activities may take the same amount of time to complete, but choosing just one or two of the important ones can result in up to 10 times the results you can get from any of the other tasks. Successful people are very good at identifying these important tasks and doing them '*no matter what*' according to research by Jinalee and Singh, 2018 [20]

"Tomorrow is often the busiest day of the week." – Anonymous

Four Hour Power Hours

As a consultant, my goal now is to work four hours a day productively on my business. Four hours, that's all you need, that's a 20 hour week so it's not that you're not working all the hours but instead you give yourself some focused time. For two hours you can choose and plan tasks like reading, brainstorming, updating your website/social media, branding,

---

[20] *https://www.researchgate.net/publication/327890577_A_descriptive_study_of_time_management_models_and_theories*

marketing, writing content, getting in touch with clients, looking online, everything else can then feed into your day but make sure you get four hours of concentrated work. Trust me, this will be easy because a lot of us spend days not doing, but simply *thinking about doing*. If you do have a day job, then perhaps you can manage two hours a day. I know people who run a business alongside a full-time job. I studied four hours a day for over a year with two small children and a full-time job. And I know I'm not unique. So, where there's a will, there's a way.

The moment that I took control, and I decided I wanted two slots of two hours every day, especially Monday to Friday, everything changed because I knew all I needed to do was concentrate for those four hours in a day and I can do that. It's better than thinking that you're going to work for seven days straight, it can be tough to commit to that and it may not be sustainable.

And my reward for taking action and not allowing myself to become distracted? I like to treat myself to something. I collect a lot of newspapers, the Metro, Evening Standard, and have stashes of them. Part of my reward is going through them picking out phrases, adverts and clippings to enrich my writing. I also do other rewarding things, experiences such as shopping, visiting a place of interest or meeting up with friends.

The more organised you are, the more time you will have for those things that you really enjoy, that make you creative, that energise you when you're not working.

It would appear, though, that certain kinds of distraction are good. In a study published in the *Journal of Consumer*

Research (Ravi Metha et al.),[21] it was shown that some low-level noise can create a distraction that can help you to think imaginatively. It even suggests that going out of one's comfort zone into a noisier place activates creative ideas in the brain, so perhaps you might want to find a new work space if you're struggling to get started or make traction on that project.

Dealing with Email

There are ways to deal with email effectively if you don't want to become inundated. I rarely go into my email box first thing in the morning because I believe most of the emails there are going to take away some of my time and, more importantly, my focus during those crucial first two hours of concentration during my working day. Similarly, I don't go on social media first thing in the morning. I try to visit my email inbox twice a day and have made a point of not connecting my work emails to my phone. My job is expendable. I am not. Work emails have been described as digital handcuffs.

Is email the greatest ever invention or greatest distraction tool ever created?

The system I'm trying to adopt with my email is what I call the 3-D system – delete, delegate or do it now. It's difficult for me to read an email and respond to it straight away because many do entail further attention that also has to be organised and integrated into my work. However, I try to delete those that I have no interest in and you should do that too, otherwise they just clog up your inbox.

---

[21] https://www.jstor.org/stable/*10*.1086/665048?origin=JSTOR-pdf&seq=1#metadata_info_tab_contents

If you've subscribed to anything and you haven't read what they've sent you in the last three months, it's time to delete those emails and unsubscribe. If you do want to pick up that relationship again at some point, you can always subscribe later on.

I have a separate business email address so that I know most of the emails that come into that inbox are important. I also have a different email that I use for newsletters I subscribe to, so when something comes in I can check if it's something interesting and relevant. I can put time aside later to go through it if need be, otherwise I can just delete it straight away.

Dealing with Social Media

I remember when I first joined Facebook, I was one of those who was totally addicted to the platform. This was around the time of the downturn in the economy, so my business was actually slowing down and, just to make time pass more quickly, I'd spend more time than was necessary on Facebook. That was the first social media to make such an impact then, so I spent quite a lot of time there – that and the Daily Mail website, which is the holy grail of celebrity gossip. Those two competed for my attention almost every day for weeks, so when I started weaning myself off them, it was quite difficult. It's hard to believe that that was almost 13 years ago. How time flies.

To wean myself off this addiction, I used an app called SelfControl to help me reduce my online activity and control my online surfing..."the rabbit hole" of the internet. It has worked because my online ferreting has reduced, I now search for fewer things and I visit sites for a much shorter time than I used to.

Attacking the Online Gremlins

What you do with the SelfControl[22] app is enter a particular website's URL along with the amount of time you want to be blocked from accessing that website, could be four hours or eight hours – you choose – so, if you do go to visit that website, you'll be unable to login. I started locking myself out between 9 and 5 at first and after about three months I was able to wean myself off distractions online. I honestly can't remember the last time I've spent up to an hour on Facebook. When I do login, whoever comes up on my homepage I'll like, congratulate or wish them a happy birthday and then go to exactly what I need to do. Because we also manage Facebook for some clients, I can go through the backend without having to see my personal profile, so that makes me more effective.

"Do what you need to do so you can do what you want to do" is my mantra.

---

[22] https://selfcontrolapp.com/

CHAPTER TEN

MASTERING MOTIVATION

Ideas. Where Do They Come from?

Perhaps you went abroad, visited a bakery and you fell in love with the pastry. You simply loved the idea of it all because you'd always wanted to set up your own food shop. This is Hummingbird's story and how a visit to a New York Patisserie sparked the hugely successful bakery chain which boasts one of the best red velvet birthday cakes in London – I can vouch for that.

So, next time when you have a thought like this yourself, depending on your experiences and passions, you may want to check out the idea and perhaps attend some training courses on it and add something different by putting your own twist on it. Remember, it doesn't have to be something groundbreaking, it could just be something that you've added your own flavour to. No pun intended.

Motivation

Although mostly positive, motivation could also be inspired by an unpleasant experience. Maybe you grew up somewhere where you were unhappy because you were denied things that your friends took for granted or you grew up in a place where you never got to eat the kind of things you would have liked.

Could this be the sort of impetus that you need in order to change or adapt?

With my own young family, I wanted to make sure they had those things I didn't have. Growing up, I shared a room with my three brothers and so it was important to me that my children had their own space in our home.

"Cherish your visions and your dreams as they are the children of your soul, the blueprints of your ultimate achievements." – Napoleon Hill

This is where you find some people invest a lot in private education for their children, buying them the best clothes, toys and going on holidays because they are probably coming from a place of pain with a childhood that wasn't that great. So, whatever it is that inspires you or motivates you to achieve your vision or your goal, use it now.

In my first book, *Unleash Your Business MOJO!,* I wrote about how I use music to motivate and inspire me. I have some tracks that I play when I feel down, and these help me to re-focus my energy and give me the impetus to carry on and keep going. You could try this too!

Remember, to feel truly motivated, it has to be all about something you really want. You can't set your own vision or goals around someone else's. For instance, maybe your parents wanted you to be something when you grew up and then you've held onto this dream or vision, but it simply won't work. When I was a child, my parents' goal for me was to be a doctor, lawyer or accountant so, to fulfil my parents', or rather my father's dream of what they wanted me to be, I chose to be an accountant but I haven't really enjoyed being an accountant because of some of the tasks involved and it can be monotonous. Whilst I am numerate, working with figures all day long is not my idea of fun.

Freedom to Fly

I also love my freedom and I like to think laterally with no boundaries and that's something that accounting does not really allow me to do. It's a bit of a fuddy-duddy profession (respect to those who love it!). So, whatever it is for you, make sure it's your dream and something you like. I chose to pivot in this direction, not because it was my dream, I was living my father's dream.

Twenty, even ten years, ago teaching enterprise and entrepreneurial management would not even have been an option but now we, as educators in this domain, are in demand. I'm hoping to take this further and do more by taking advantage of the online and offline opportunities that I am now being exposed to. That's my motivation.

CHAPTER ELEVEN

VALUE YOURSELF

Your Worth

What are you worth? Value your time. Now, because we're talking about time, time is a finite resource – everybody gets 24 hours a day and when it's gone, it's gone. You can't add any more seconds or minutes to the 24 hours that we're given so, in order for us to make sure that we're making the right choices, we need to put a value on what we're working for, i.e. paid as if you are in a salaried job.

Research shows that if you earn more money, you are more likely to eat better, exercise better, live a better quality life and get better medical care. So we do need money, it's essential to living a better life.

> *Determine exactly how much you earn each hour and what you have to do to increase your hourly rate in the months and years ahead.*

Put Some Metrics on Your Time

Keep it simple. All you need to do is work out how many hours you work in a week, or a year, and just divide that by how much you get paid and that gives your hourly rate – you get paid £700 a week doing 35 hours so that's £20 per hour.

When you're thinking of doing something different, you can take that rate into account. If you're self- employed, you can work this out based on what you earn and the number of hours you put into each one of your projects.

If someone asks you to do something and is going to pay you, decide if the rate they're offering is worth your time and then make up your mind.

"I'm a great believer in luck, and I find the harder I work the more I have of it." – Thomas Jefferson

Invest Time for Future Rewards

However, if someone asks you to do something for free and you think that there might be potential to earn more because of future work as a result of the opportunity to improve your skills in a particular area, then at least that will be your choice. That's an example of how you can choose between two options. Besides, it could also be a great networking opportunity.

If you feel that your hourly rate is low based on your vision and goals for the future, then this is where you can start to work towards what you want. You need to identify those things you can do to make sure you earn more.

As I said earlier, this could include training yourself up to get a new qualification, moving jobs, asking for a pay rise. This will depend on the job you're doing because if you're an administrative officer, there's only so much you can earn, so you may need to retrain or start to look for a new job to achieve career progression. I saw this quote once, "*You learn first then you remove the L and earn*"

Learn Online

In this day and age of online training and learning, you can upskill yourself by registering for an online course and get qualified. I know people who have changed jobs by just watching a few YouTube videos.

And guess what? You could become an instructor or teacher online too. Is there something you're good at that you can begin to train others in? Could you write a manual about that? Start to think of those latent skills you have that could probably produce more money.

> *"Identify the self-limiting beliefs that you have. How would you act if they were completely untrue?"*

You see, our minds are the most powerful engine we have, they are also simple to adjust. You should watch this programme if you can, *Can Derren Brown Help You Overcome Your Fears? Fear and Faith* (2012)[23]. Part one is on YouTube and it's a ground-breaking demonstration of how powerful our subconscious minds are.

Look into things that you might have wanted to do in the past. For example, if it's investing in property, do you know anybody who can show you how to do that? Start looking for ideas/opportunities that can help you to get from where you are now to where you want to be.

---

[23] https://www.youtube.com/watch?v=U4RxtyuFezs&ab_channel=DerrenBrown

MOJO'S TIPS

Make a list of 10 things that you would like to do if money were no object.

1.

2.

3.

4.

5.

6.

7.

8.

9.

10.

Delegating

Look at the activities that you do that are low-level and get somebody else to do those chores for much less than your hourly rate. For instance, if your hourly rate is £75 and yet you find yourself doing things like responding to mundane emails and doing basic admin tasks, you can always get somebody to do these for much less. This means you spend your time doing those high quality and high-level activities that are bringing in more money. Think of delegating those tasks that are repetitive and require less skill.

This also applies to chores in the house so, when you start making enough money, look around the house, identify those tasks that you know someone else can do, this could be cleaning, gardening or ironing (I hate this with a passion). This frees your mind from having to worry about those chores so you can concentrate on the things that matter more.

CHAPTER TWELVE

THE MATRIX RELOADED

Navigating the Time Matrix

In his book, *The Seven Habits of Highly Effective People*, Steve Covey[24] talks about the time management matrix which divides tasks up into four main quadrants as explained below:

Details	Urgent	Not Urgent
Important	**Quadrant 1:** Urgent and important activities: deadlines and meetings	**Quadrant 3:** Important but not urgent activities: personal and business goals
Not important	**Quadrant 2:** Urgent but not important activities: gossiping notifications or emails	**Quadrant 4:** Not urgent and not important activities: excessive TV or social media

[24] *Covey, Steve 2003. The Seven Habits of Highly Effective People. FranklinCovey*

Quadrant I

The first is the urgent and important quadrant. This contains things that have to be done right now as they have become a crisis. These include pressing problems, deadlines that are now due or overdue, last-minute preparations, exam cramming and emergencies that could have been done earlier – think of a dripping tap that becomes a big leak, destroying property and costing money. In this quadrant, we become firefighters dealing with issues that should have been taken care of before now.

Quadrant II

The second quadrant focuses on tasks that are urgent but not important. This could be a telephone ringing, notifications on your phone, some meetings. Something may appear to need your attention, but you have to ask yourself – is it really important? You'll need to decide if it is and if it requires you to break away from your priorities. In this day and age, we have so much that distracts us, such as social media, so all this needs to be kept to a minimum so we can focus on what's important for us now. Other people's problems or issues form part of this quadrant too. Emails are often someone else's agenda, and they tend to take you away from yours. I am very mindful of skating around in my inbox. Of course, if you have to and it's work related, do attend to them but otherwise, if you have something that you are working on, then you have no business checking your emails or WhatsApp messages every minute as I discussed earlier.

"What is important is seldom urgent and what is urgent is seldom important." – Dwight D. Eisenhower

Quadrant III

The third quadrant contains tasks that are important but not urgent. These are the ones that we find the hardest to do, and this is where the magic really happens. Right now, they appear not to be really important, but we need to work on these every day, every week and every month. This is where we take action on our personal goals and our vision for the future. They may not seem urgent now because they're not directly influencing the goals that we need to act upon, plan and schedule for. This includes relationship building, searching for new opportunities, planning for the children, preventative activities like looking after our health, planned study, setting goals for the future, investing in all those activities which, if not dealt with, become urgent and important – quadrant one activities.

Quadrant IV

The final quadrant is packed with activities that we really enjoy doing. Watching TV, surfing the net, social media, gossiping, they all waste time and are generally unnecessary. We need to cut these activities to a minimum. We need to be aware of the time we spend doing these and try to reduce it.

A lot of the things we sometimes do are actually firefighting and these are things that are urgent and important like a bill that you knew was due, but you didn't take the time to pay it; now today you're rushing around but you've misplaced your card, you can't get onto your online banking and now you're stressed because a late payment fee might be applied. All this could have been prevented if you'd paid it promptly or set up a payment system or set a reminder. We need to reduce our firefighting. Getting your car insurance at least a month before it's due can actually save you money, for example.

We find ourselves rushing around to complete things at the last minute, like coursework back in school – you knew that assignment was due on a particular day three months ago and yet you did nothing and then there you were, in the last few days, struggling to complete it. Some of us kid ourselves that we work better under pressure and the creative juices flow at the last minute and, whilst that could be true, it's still additional pressure. Although the body can deal with some stress, too much of it is not good for us, so beware and try to plan ahead of time.

Conclusion

"The End is the beginning" – Winston Churchill

As I come to the end of this book, at the beginning of 2021, we are still firmly in the middle of the pandemic, which has gripped us and left us more worried and stressed about what lies beyond. I know these are trying times and the future seems uncertain. However, research has shown that entrepreneurs and visionaries actually thrive in circumstances such as these.

To paraphrase Ralph W Emerson, *"What lies within us is greater than what lies before or behind us."*

This has been a difficult time, and I have coped with it by watching a lot less news. I can say I have never actually watched a news story on any of the media channels. I stick to reading a few extracts on my phone, which is more than enough to keep me updated. I find the news distracting and depressing. Being a survivor of the 2007 economic crash, I decided never to watch the main news channels, and I have kept to that and kept my sanity as well. I read news on my phone, at times I can control.

My top tip for managing your time and avoiding procrastination is to revisit your vision and your goals, at least once a month to help you keep on track. Try to start the week with just three goals/tasks that you want to achieve. You must focus on tasks that are moving you towards your goals. Not having an aim leads to despair.

And please do not go with the "all or nothing approach" where, just because you didn't do great with one particular goal, it's all over, like being on a weight loss programme and eating a bar of chocolate on day five and then throwing in the towel. Acknowledge that you are human and that it's about the journey as well as the destination.

Great wins are awesome but they are quite rare. You get a lot more from small wins. According to research by Anabile and Kramer in their book, *The Progress Principle: Using small wins to Ignite Joy, Engagement and Creativity at Work*[25], they assert that setting clear and meaningful goals will boost our emotions and motivate us to do better.

"Be not afraid of going slowly, be afraid only of standing still." – Chinese proverb

I for one have set some small goals and a few major ones. One of those main goals was to lose that extra weight that I've been carrying around for years. I set my goals, using spreadsheets and apps to keep me on track. Yes, I measured everything to ensure that my goals and tasks could be managed and tweaked. What does not get measured cannot get managed, and therefore goals might become difficult to achieve. I celebrated my wins, sometimes that was no weight loss (but no weight gain) for that week. I was able to look at my food

---

[25] *Kramer and Anabile, 2011. The Progress Principle: Using small wins to Ignite Joy, Engagement and Creativity at Work. Harvard Business Review Press.*

for that week and make tweaks, I kept it up and I'm now 12 kgs lighter.

"What gets measured gets managed."

Research shows that being happy leads you to be optimistic about achieving your goals, and not that achieving goals makes you happy. Showing gratitude and being able to explain why you want to achieve your goals and the difference it will make to you is important. In *Creating your Best Life*, Caroline A Miller[26] actually went further to state that you should spend 20 minutes for three days writing about your future life as if all your goals had gone to plan. Also, get that subconscious mind to work while you're getting on with life - use words from your goals as your passwords, they should be easy to remember and also double up as a reminder of what you want in your life.

Thank you for reading this book and if you found it useful please leave a review so others can also benefit from it.

I wish you a happy and successful future. Be sure to reach out to me on social media.

Poem adapted from *Don't Quit* by John Greenleaf Whittier (1807 - 1892)

Rest, if you must, but don't quit.

Don't give up though the pace seems slow.

---

[26] *Miller Caroline A, 2011. Creating your Best Life. Sterling.*

You may succeed with another blow.

It may be near when it seems so far.

So stick to the fight when you're hardest hit.

It's when things seem worst that you must not QUIT.

One Last Thing…

If you enjoyed this book or found it useful I'd be very grateful if you'd post a short review on Amazon. Your support really does make a difference and I read all the reviews personally. Your feedback will make this book and the resources that I provide even better.

To your success.

Mojo x

Printed in Great Britain
by Amazon

24334220R00050